# LOS ANGELES KINGS

BY ETHAN OLSON

Book design by Maggie Villaume
Cover design by Maggie Villaume

Photographs ©: Ashley Landis/AP Images, cover; Jae C. Hong/AP Images, 4–5; Duncan Williams/Cal Sport Media/AP Images, 7; Mark J. Terrill/AP Images, 8, 27, 29; AP Images, 10–11; Mark Avery/AP Images, 12; Pugliese/AP Images, 15; Reed Saxon/AP Images, 16–17; Paul Connors/AP Images, 18; Jason Redmond/AP Images, 21; Kostas Lymperopoulos/Cal Sport Media/AP Images, 23; Tim Warner/Cal Sport Media/AP Images, 24–25

Press Box Books, an imprint of Press Room Editions.

**ISBN**
978-1-63494-675-9 (library bound)
978-1-63494-699-5 (paperback)
978-1-63494-745-9 (epub)
978-1-63494-723-7 (hosted ebook)

**Library of Congress Control Number: 2022919283**

Distributed by North Star Editions, Inc.
2297 Waters Drive
Mendota Heights, MN 55120
www.northstareditions.com

Printed in the United States of America
Mankato, MN
082023

## ABOUT THE AUTHOR
Ethan Olson is a sportswriter and editor based in Minneapolis.

# TABLE OF CONTENTS

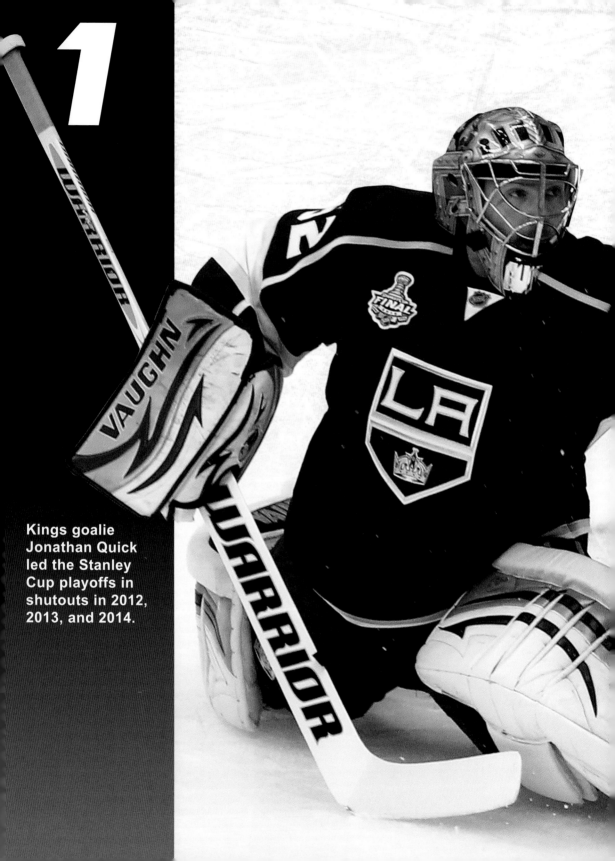

**1**

Kings goalie Jonathan Quick led the Stanley Cup playoffs in shutouts in 2012, 2013, and 2014.

By 2012, the Los Angeles Kings had been in the National Hockey League (NHL) for 43 seasons. They had yet to win a Stanley Cup. And that didn't seem likely to change heading into the 2012 playoffs.

Eight teams in each conference make the playoffs. The Kings were the eighth seed in the Western Conference. To pull a postseason upset, the Kings needed their stars to step up. Goalie Jonathan Quick did just that.

Quick was lights out in the first two rounds. He allowed only 14 goals in nine games. His best performance was a 41-save shutout. That came against the Vancouver Canucks in Game 3 of the first round. And as the playoffs continued, Quick kept coming up big.

Game 5 of the conference finals went to overtime tied 3–3. Quick helped keep the game tied. In the third period, a Phoenix Coyotes winger hit Quick while he was making a save. Then while Quick was spread out on the ice, he reached out his glove to catch another shot. The Kings won 4–3 in overtime.

Quick prepares to make one of his 32 saves in Game 2 of the 2012 Stanley Cup Final.

They faced the New Jersey Devils in the Stanley Cup Final. The Kings jumped out to a 2–0 series lead. They returned

Quick hoists the Stanley Cup in 2012.

to Los Angeles for Game 3. Quick was at his best once again. He stopped 22 shots to record his third shutout of the playoffs.

Three games later, the Kings clinched the championship at home.

Quick's performance throughout the playoffs earned him the Conn Smythe Trophy. That trophy is given to the best player of the playoffs each year. Quick helped the Kings make their mark in NHL history. And they weren't done yet.

## • RECORD-SETTING PLAYOFF RUN

The Kings became the first number eight seed in NHL history to beat the top three seeds in their conference. But that isn't the only record they set. No number eight seed had ever won a championship in any of the major North American professional men's leagues before. Only one other eight seed reached the Stanley Cup Final before the Kings. The Edmonton Oilers did in 2006, but they lost to the Carolina Hurricanes.

**2**

Starting in 1967, the Kings played in the Forum for 32 years.

# HUMBLE BEGINNINGS

**T**he Kings made their NHL debut in 1967–68. But they didn't have a permanent home yet. The "Fabulous Forum" opened two months into their first season and became their home arena for decades. They finished that year second in the West Division. The Kings were knocked out in the first round of the playoffs.

The early success didn't last. The Kings missed the playoffs four

The Kings' Marcel Dionne (16) celebrates a teammate's goal in a December 1986 game.

years straight to start the 1970s. Things started to look up after Los Angeles traded for center Marcel Dionne in 1975.

Dionne was a star right away. His first season with the Kings saw him put up 94 points. He got even better when Bob Berry became the coach in 1978–79. Berry paired Dionne with wingers Dave Taylor and Charlie Simmer. The trio became known as the "Triple Crown Line." Dionne provided the playmaking. Taylor and

## •MIRACLE ON MANCHESTER

The Forum hosted the largest comeback in NHL playoff history in 1982. It was Game 3 of the opening round. With the series tied 1–1, the Edmonton Oilers jumped out to a 5–0 lead. And it was only the second period. Los Angeles scored five goals in the third period to send the game to overtime. Then a Daryl Evans slap shot won it for the Kings.

Simmer scored off Dionne's great passing. Together, they became one of the best scoring combinations in NHL history.

Taylor played his entire career in Los Angeles. But Dionne and Simmer were both gone by 1987. The Kings played in a city known for its stars. And they needed a new one. They got the biggest star in the league when they traded for Wayne Gretzky in 1988. The move shocked the hockey world. "The Great One" won his ninth Hart Memorial Trophy during his first season with the Kings. That award goes to the league's most valuable player.

The team started to reach new heights with Gretzky. They peaked in 1992–93. Gretzky and Luc Robitaille led the Kings to

Wayne Gretzky (99) scores his 800th NHL goal during a March 1994 game.

their first Stanley Cup Final. Los Angeles lost to the Montreal Canadiens in five games. But a new standard had been set.

# 3

Luc Robitaille
celebrates
scoring for the
Kings in a 1993
playoff game.

# BIG-CITY COMEBACK

**T**he 1993 playoff run gave hope to many Kings fans. But in the following years, the team ran into money issues. Owner Bruce McNall had been spending big for years. Losing money caught up with him. McNall sold the team in 1994. New owners Philip Anschutz and Edward Roski still had to make cuts. The biggest was trading Wayne Gretzky in 1996.

Ziggy Pálffy tallied 340 points with the Kings from 1999 to 2004.

The changes didn't stop there.
The Kings left the Forum in 1999 after
32 seasons. Their new home was the

Staples Center in downtown Los Angeles. The Kings made the playoffs in their first season playing there. Players like Luc Robitaille and Ziggy Pálffy gave the fans much to cheer about. But they were knocked out in the first round.

The Kings made the playoffs the next two years as well. But their luck soon changed. Robitaille left after the 2000–01 season. After 2002, the Kings missed the playoffs for six straight seasons.

## •UNEXPECTED BREAKUP

Rob Blake played 14 years of his Hall of Fame career with the Kings. He was beloved by Los Angeles fans. In 2001, the team traded him to the Colorado Avalanche. It became worse for Kings fans when they met the Avalanche in that year's playoffs. The Avalanche won in seven games. Blake went on to lift the Stanley Cup with Colorado that year.

Los Angeles rebuilt through the draft. During that time, the Kings picked players like forwards Dustin Brown and Anze Kopitar. They also got defenseman Drew Doughty and goaltender Jonathan Quick. Those four players became key pieces to the Kings' success.

By 2009–10, the Kings had improved. They finished with 101 points. That was only their third season with more than 100 points. They continued to make the playoffs. But a change was needed after two early playoff exits. They decided to fire their head coach during the 2011–12 season. Things changed for the better when the team hired Darryl Sutter as the replacement.

Jonathan Quick (left) and Drew Doughty celebrate a
Kings win during the 2009–10 season.

# JONATHAN QUICK

The Kings selected Jonathan Quick in the third round of the 2005 draft. Few expected the goalie from Connecticut to become one of the league's best. That changed when Quick played out of his mind in the 2012 playoffs. His star power was becoming clear. The Kings signed Quick to a 10-year contract after winning the Stanley Cup.

Quick became the team's leader in shutouts in 2014. He didn't stop there. In 2016, he broke the shutout record for American goalies. Consistency was his greatest strength.

During his dominant stretch, Quick earned two William M. Jennings Trophies. That award is given to the goalie who allows the fewest goals in the regular season.

Quick was still going strong with the Kings in 2022. And he will always be known as the star who helped Los Angeles win its first Stanley Cup.

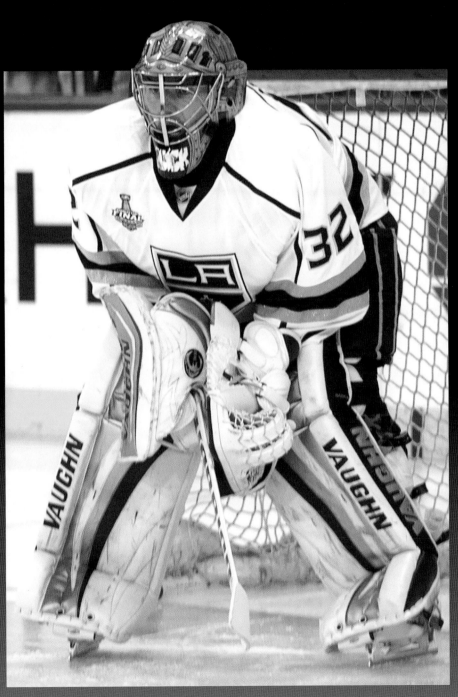

Jonathan Quick holds the Kings' records for most wins, most shutouts, and best save percentage.

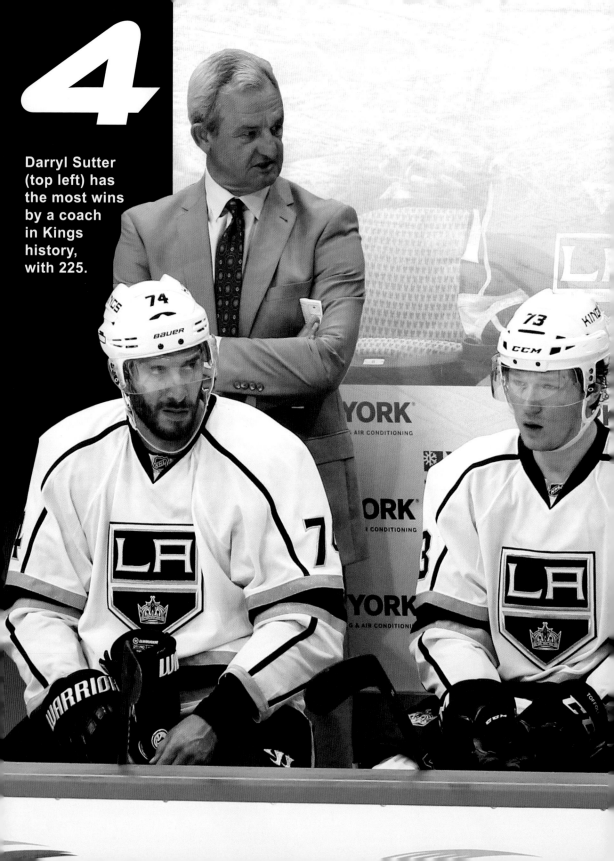

**4**

Darryl Sutter (top left) has the most wins by a coach in Kings history, with 225.

# SUTTER'S SUCCESS

**D**arryl Sutter had a track record of success. He had missed the playoffs only twice in 12 years as a head coach. His veteran leadership helped turn the Kings around quickly.

The Kings won the Stanley Cup in Sutter's first year in 2012. But they weren't done. In 2013–14, Jonathan Quick was still at the top of his game. Drew Doughty was one of the NHL's best defensemen.

And center Anze Kopitar was a dangerous scorer. He led the team with 70 points that season.

The Kings had to battle in the 2014 playoffs. They fell behind the San Jose Sharks 3–0 in the first round. The Kings came back to beat San Jose 5–1 on the road in Game 7. They became the fourth team ever to overcome a 3–0 series deficit.

Their next two series also went to seven games. Defenseman Alec Martinez scored in overtime in Game 7 of the conference finals. That sent the Kings back to the Stanley Cup Final.

Martinez came up big again in the Cup Final against the New York Rangers.

Anze Kopitar led the playoffs in scoring in both 2012 and 2014.

The Kings were up 3–1 in the series heading into Game 5 in Los Angeles. The game went to double overtime. After a Kings rush up the ice, center Tyler Toffoli had his shot saved. Martinez was in the perfect position for the rebound. His second overtime goal of the playoffs secured another Cup for the Kings.

The team started to decline after that championship. The Kings missed the playoffs in two of the next three years. Sutter was fired after the 2016–17 season.

Team legends like Quick, Doughty, and Kopitar stuck around, though. They led the Kings back to the playoffs

## •A NEW HOME

The Forum was close to many Kings fans' hearts. But memories were soon made in the Staples Center. The downtown Los Angeles arena hosted the games that won the Kings both of their Stanley Cups. It also helped bring more fans to games. The average attendance increased from almost 12,800 to more than 16,500 after the move.

**Alec Martinez celebrates his overtime winner in Game 5 of the 2014 Stanley Cup Final.**

in 2022. Fans were hopeful that core still had another Cup run in them.

# LOS ANGELES KINGS
## QUICK STATS

**TEAM HISTORY:** Los Angeles Kings (1967–)

**STANLEY CUP CHAMPIONSHIPS:** 2 (2012, 2014)

**KEY COACHES:**

• Bob Pulford (1972–77): 178 wins, 150 losses, 68 ties

• Barry Melrose (1992–95): 79 wins, 101 losses, 29 ties

• Darryl Sutter (2011–17): 225 wins, 147 losses,
  53 overtime losses

**HOME ARENA:** Crypto.com Arena (Los Angeles, CA)

**MOST CAREER POINTS:** Marcel Dionne (1,307)

**MOST CAREER GOALS:** Luc Robitaille (557)

**MOST CAREER ASSISTS:** Marcel Dionne (757)

**MOST CAREER SHUTOUTS:** Jonathan Quick (56)

*Stats are accurate through the 2021–22 season.*

# GLOSSARY

**CONFERENCE**
A smaller group of teams that make up part of a sports league.

**DRAFT**
An event that allows teams to choose new players coming into a league.

**OVERTIME**
One or more extra periods played after regulation if a game is still tied.

**REBOUND**
When the goalie makes a save, but the puck goes back into play.

**SERIES**
A number of games played in a row between the same two teams.

**SHUTOUT**
A game in which a team does not allow a goal.

**VETERAN**
A player or coach who has spent several years in a league.

# TO LEARN MORE

## BOOKS

Davidson, B. Keith. *NHL*. New York: Crabtree Publishing, 2022.

Doeden, Matt. *G.O.A.T. Hockey Teams*. Minneapolis: Lerner Publications, 2021.

Ryan, Mike. *Hockey Now! The Biggest Stars of the NHL*. Buffalo, NY: Firefly Books, 2022.

## MORE INFORMATION

To learn more about the Los Angeles Kings, go to **pressboxbooks.com/AllAccess**.

These links are routinely monitored and updated to provide the most current information available.

## INDEX